How to
Forget your ex

with the stab of a fork

D1407874

© 2007 Rebo International
This edition: © 2007 Rebo Productions b.v., Lisse

www.rebo-publishers.com
info@rebo-publishers.com

Text: Claire Jacquet en Marina Veuillet
Photography: Raphaële Vidaling
Design: Claire Guigal
Original title: Comment oublier son ex d'un bon coup de fourchette
Translation: Nannie Nieland-Weits
Editing: Studio Imago, Amersfoort

ISBN 978-90-366-2173-1

So it's time to get a grip on the present again, refocus your shambolic life on the one important certainty: YOU ARE ALIVE! Enjoy every moment, savor it, nibble away at it, lick your lips; life is for eating!

The aim of this book is to get you to rediscover the pleasures of life, starting with the pleasure of eating. Your desires are probably very basic (sweet/savory, mild/spicy), or maybe linked to textures (smooth/crunchy). Food was the first victim of your new, solitary life, but it will also be the first way of finding satisfaction, because it's readily accessible. Cooking starts by providing food for our senses. Whether it's choosing products from a display, getting the cooking time just right, admiring a pretty plate, or treating yourself to a slap-up meal, the senses of sight, touch, hearing, smell, and taste are put to work. So cooking is very therapeutic—it occupies the hands and the mind, proves your ability to work a few minor miracles, and, once you've got your confidence back, your ability to make up your own versions of certain recipes to give them a personal touch.

Your routine has been interrupted, but take advantage of your unaccustomed situation. It's an opportunity to make the most of your newfound freedom and indulge yourself with a few gastronomic pranks. It's up to you to listen to your own needs. The guiding principle is, "Spoil yourself, because you're worth it!"

The French poet Lamartine lamented that if one person is missing from your life, the whole world seems empty. So fill up your life again, starting with your plate…

Great romantic movies

There's nothing like a good romantic movie for reconciling you to your existence and restoring your belief in total, unconditional love. Besides, it's always easier when you're not involved anymore. Well hardly… because some screenplays bear a strange resemblance to real life, despite the well-known formula "Any similarity to any real person is purely coincidental, etc.," so much so that they turn into strange trailers that, consciously or unconsciously, act like mirrors, mimicking the relationships of couples in free-fall. When words fail, movies are still there to express the unthinkable or the inconceivable. The studios are yours!

Romantic movies with happy endings

- *La Belle Nivernaise:* Jean Epstein
- *Sunrise and City Girl:* Friedrich Wilhelm Murnau
- *The Shining Hour:* Frank Borzage
- *Lonesome:* Paul Fejos
- *City Lights:* Charles Chaplin
- *L'Atalante:* Jean Vigo
- *An Affair to Remember:* Leo McCarey
- *Rebecca:* Alfred Hitchcock
- *Meet John Doe:* Frank Capra
- *I Know Where I'm Going and A Matter of Life and Death:* Michael Powell and Emeric Pressburger
- *The Ghost and Mrs. Muir:* Joseph L. Mankiewicz
- *Magnificent Obsession and All that Heaven Allows:* Douglas Sirk

- *Lumière d'été:* Jean Grémillon
- *To Have and Have Not:* Howard Hawks
- *To Joy:* Ingmar Bergman
- *Pandora and the Flying Dutchman:* Albert Lewin
- *The Quiet Man:* John Ford
- *Voyage to Italy:* Roberto Rossellini
- *River of no Return:* Otto Preminger
- *Lola:* Jacques Demy
- *The Immortal Story:* Orson Welles

- *Minnie and Moskowitz:* John Cassavetes
- *Pakeezah (Pure Heart):* Kamal Amrohi
- *The French Lieutenant's Woman:* Karel Reisz
- *The Green Ray:* Éric Rohmer
- *Children of a Lesser God:* Randa Haines
- *Always:* Steven Spielberg
- *Les Amants du Pont-Neuf:* Léos Carax
- *Tie me up! Tie me Down!:* Pedro Almodovar
- *The Man without a Past:* Aki Kaurismaki

Romantic movies with sad endings

- *Morocco:* Josef von Sternberg
- *Back Street:* John Stahl
- *One Way Passage:* Tay Garnett
- *Duel in the Sun:* King Vidor
- *Brief Encounter, Doctor Zhivago, and Ryan's Daughter:* David Lean
- *Written in the Wind, The Tarnished Angels, and The Time to Love and the Time to Die:* Douglas Sirk
- *Splendor in the Grass:* Elia Kazan
- *They Live by Night:* Nicholas Ray
- *Liebelei:* Max Ophuls
- *The Crucified Lovers:* Kenji Mizoguchi
- *Pierrot le Fou:* Jean-Luc Godard
- *Jules et Jim and The Woman Next Door:* François Truffaut
- *The Other:* Youssef Chahine
- *Oblomov:* Nikita Mikhalkov
- *Fear Eats the Soul:* Rainer Werner Fassbinder
- *Body to Heart:* Paul Vecchiali

Pampering myself more than he/she ever did

Recipes for cocooning: light, sweet, or slightly tart

Nobody loves me

Still full of anxiety, frightened of being alone with only yourself for company, you feel like you've been dumped by the roadside, thrown out like an old plant that has dried up in its pot… If you deserve to have fate strike you such a blow, it must be because you are no longer interesting, or worth looking at, so you must be even less desirable than an old boot. You're incapable of thinking coherently or concentrating on anything for more than ten seconds, and you've reached the stage when you can't even rebel any more.

And yet… Who knows you inside and out? Who knows exactly what you like, and when and how? Who knows every detail about you? Why, you, of course, and nobody else!

So don't give up on yourself! And as pleasures slip away when troubles disrupt your life, indulge yourself with all the simple luxuries you can enjoy at home, starting with a bath. It's the first step on the road to recovery (one of the top remedies in the first aid box for broken hearts). The

water gently enfolds you, bearing your weight so you float like a feather on the surface. Besides, it's one of the few things you can rely on at the moment, so make the most of it. Restored to your former self by the weightlessness of this substitute for amniotic fluid, think of the small things that might make any future regressions to the womb even more pleasant, like bath foam or relaxing essential oils (neroli, marjoram, bitter orange, tangerine…), or a few candles instead of that unforgiving electric light, or even some delicious little chocolates to eat while listening to music or reading…

Now you're almost back in shape, ready to go out, do a bit of shopping, find the right places to put the things you've bought, and use them to change the landscape around you. Move a few odds and ends or a lamp, then go for the furniture, change the shape of the bedroom, hang up some photos… In this first phase of rebuilding, take particular care over the colors surrounding you, as they affect your state of mind. White cleanses the spirit, yellow warms it, pink flatters it, red stimulates it, while black plunges it into despair… You will be writing the sequel to the movie, and the colors that go with it!

Incidentally, while we're on the subject, choose films that are full of energy (see p. 10) and have a happy ending, if possible. Misery is contagious. It's better to watch musical comedies that will fill you with a dizzying passion for life. The characters may go through a few sticky patches, but they still end up with dancing in the streets… Will you get that far?

This stage is about getting back to basics. There's nothing left on the battlefield, except you, to record the scale of the disaster. Well, after all, that's not so bad, since you're the one who needs looking after. This is the first step, and that's why the recipes in this chapter are simple and comforting.

Good resolutions

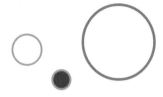

New interior
Does the ghost of your ex still haunt your flat? Change your interior, in all senses of the word! Change the color of a wall (just one coat of paint in the right place), buy that designer lamp you've always dreamed of, place a weekly order with your local florist...

Blinkers going cheap
And if what hurts is the old routine, the routine from before the break-up, change your habits! Did you usually have coffee in a particular coffee-hop? Go to the one opposite! Did you read a certain magazine every week? Try another one. Give up the car or the subway and explore your town by bicycle. At all events, take an alternative route—that way lies salvation.

Scents
The best advice we can give you when you change course is to change your perfume. Every time in your life has its own olfactory memory card. Perhaps you used to be "In Love Again" "Trouble"... Before the disaster, he gave "Miracle," but the miracle didn't work. And you're probably more "Opium" or "Pure Poiso. Unless you go more for the mysterious blend of "Odeur from Comme des Garçons, which conjures up the scents of dry washing, sand dunes, metal, oxygen, and nail polish, all at th same time: guaranteed Zen serenity.

Life is rosy…
Flowers are for looking at and
smelling, but they can also be eaten…
Be brave and try "edible romanticism"!
When making a salad, for example, mix some
nasturtiums—just two or three, they have a very
strong, hot flavor—with a few leaves of lettuce and
endive, and season with raspberry vinegar and
olive oil.

Of love and fresh water
You have just realized that you
cannot live on love and fresh water
alone. "Sloppy films and booze" are better
company at the moment. But enjoy them in
moderation all the same and start a regular plain
water cure with a few glasses of sparkling water. It's
bright and "cool," like the Colette Water-Bar in
Paris, which suggests you drink lots of mineral
water to sober up after melancholy evenings.
After taking this cure, you'll be ready for
anything: with a clear head, a light
heart, and ready to take on all
comers.

Cheerful salad

The time is right for innovation and experimentation of all kinds with just one end in view: to break with the grayness of everyday and put a bit of color into your life (and why not a few vitamins as well?). Without your really knowing why, reinventing the well-known tomato and feta salad suddenly becomes vaguely comforting (the desire to move on to something else?) as well as a good breath of fresh air on your plate.

Preparation time:
5 minutes

· 2 good-sized slices of watermelon
· 1 tbsp mint leaves
· 2 oz (50 g) feta cheese
· 2 tbsp fruited olive oil
· Salt and
  pepper

Peel the slices of watermelon and remove the seeds. Cut the flesh in large cubes. Set aside a few mint leaves for garnishing and chop the rest.

Mix the watermelon, feta, and chopped mint. Season with salt and pepper, drizzle with the olive oil and garnish with the remaining mint leaves. Eat well chilled.

Eggs mimosa with preserved lemons

Not ready to get your teeth into a large steak tartare yet? Here's a good alternative, recommended by our friend Clara, who on bad days climbs up on her roof like a squirrel to eat this sunny dish and think about the next children's story she's going to illustrate, while waiting for her Prince Charming... who must be a very slow young man indeed!

Preparation time: 15 minutes

· 2 eggs
· 2 preserved lemons
· 3 scallions
· Pepper

Wash the eggs and hard boil them by plunging them in boiling salted water for 10 minutes. Allow them to cool in cold water. Chop the preserved lemons (having removed the seeds) and the scallions. Halve the eggs, remove the yolks and mash them with the lemons and scallions Cut the whites in strips and arrange on a plate with the lemon mixture. Season with pepper. There's no need to add salt, preserved lemons are already salted.

Beet salad with fresh goat's cheese

Sometimes all your plans go awry, you feel lost and need to get back to basics. Here is a dish that reminds you of the garden, the woods, and homegrown food. Remember that little spot in the country, the gang of inseparable knock-kneed friends, and the sun, the wind, life! Feeling better already, aren't you?

Preparation time: 5 minutes

· I cooked beet
· I fresh goat's cheese
· A few sprigs of flat-leaf parsley
· A few hazelnuts
· I tbsp hazelnut oil
· I/2 tbsp raspberry vinegar
· Salt and pepper

Cut the beet in thin rounds and the goat's cheese in small cubes. Chop the parsley and crush the hazelnuts. Arrange the beet and goat's cheese on a plate. Sprinkle with the hazelnuts and parsley. Mix together the oil, vinegar, and salt and pepper. Drizzle this sauce over the salad and enjoy.

Caramelized artichoke hearts with taramasalata

Confront the artichoke heart inside you! The delicate, calming colors of this recipe will reconcile you to the romantic you still remain, despite everything life has thrown at you. After all, the famous French writer Stendhal, author of The Red and the Black, followed it up with another novel The Pink and the Green, the story of a passionate woman, the female counterpart of Julien Sorel in Scarlet and Black, who was determined to take control of her own destiny...

Preparation time: 10 minutes

· Butter for frying
· 3 artichoke hearts (canned or frozen)
· 1/2 tsp superfine sugar
· 3 tsp taramasalata
· Flat-leaf parsley

Melt a little butter in a skillet. When the pan is hot and the butter has melted, brown the artichoke hearts for 4–5 minutes, turning occasionally so they are golden all over. At the very end, sprinkle the sugar over the artichokes and turn them over one more time, until the sugar melts and caramelizes. Place the artichokes on a plate and put a dollop of taramasalata on each. Top with a sprig of parsley—and that's it!

Vegetable tian with leftovers

The word "leftovers" describes the remains of a dish or a meal, scraps of food that are often stored in the refrigerator, wrapped in aluminum foil. This often happens to pieces of cheese that weren't finished off the last time you had friends to dinner, and you don't know what to do with them in your new single life… This recipe suggests a cheerful, tasty way of recycling them. It will persuade you that you can make a great deal out of almost nothing and that, in your situation, nothing never means emptiness.

Preparation time: 40 minutes

· 1 onion
· 2 tomatoes
· 1 zucchini
· Odds and ends of leftover cheese
· Salt and pepper
· Thyme
· Olive oil

Preheat the oven to 375 °F (190 °C). Peel and chop the onion and brown gently in a small skillet for a good 5 minutes until nice and golden. Place in the bottom of a small gratin dish. Wash the tomatoes and zucchini and cut them in rounds (it's a nice idea to half peel the zucchini, leaving alternate strips with and without skin along the length of the vegetable). Brown the zucchini rounds on both sides in the same skillet. Cut the cheese in slices. Then all you have to do is arrange rounds of tomato, zucchini, and slices of cheese alternately over the onion. To finish, season with salt and pepper, sprinkle with thyme and add a drop of olive oil, which can only improve the taste. Bake in the oven for 25 minutes.

Udon noodle soup

A warm, sweet recipe that brings escape within reach in record time. Admittedly, the most difficult part will probably be getting all the ingredients together, but this search will be the start of the journey (an initiation for some of you) and you will discover that something exotic may be hidden between the crackers and the dairy produce… and maybe your other half as well, why not?

Preparation time: 15 minutes

- 1 tbsp dashi powder (for making Japanese dashi soup stock)
- 1/4 lb (125 g) dry udon noodles
- Generous 1 oz (30 g) fresh tofu
- 1 stem chive
- 7 nice shrimp (preferably raw)
- 1–2 tbsp dehydrated wakame seaweed
- 1/2 tbsp miso paste
- 1 tsp mirin (Korean rice wine)
- 1 tsp soy sauce
- Salt
- Sesame oil (the kind they sell in Asian markets)
- Seven-spice chili pepper (shichimi togarashi if possible)

Bring 2 cups (500 ml) water to a boil in a large pan. Stir in the dashi powder to make a stock. In another pan, set water to boil for the udon noodles and cook according to the instructions on the package (usually 5 minutes). Meanwhile, cut the tofu in small cubes (about 3/8 inch/1 cm), chop the chive and peel the shrimp, leaving the end with the tail. Drain and rinse the noodles, and set aside in a covered serving dish in a warm place. Sprinkle the wakame seaweed into the dashi stock and simmer until soft. Plunge the shrimp in the stock, and reduce the heat before adding the miso, mirin, and soy sauce. Mix well to dissolve the miso and add the tofu. Season with salt. When the shrimp have just begun to turn pink, pour the stock with the shrimp over the udon noodles, garnish with the chives and a few drops of sesame oil and sprinkle with shichimi togarashi.

Variations

This soup forms a basis for many possible variations. The shrimp may be replaced with strips of raw beef, a beaten egg, sautéed pork, leftover chicken, etc. The garnish may be enhanced by the addition of slices of raw mushroom, broiled and chopped nori seaweed, thin strips of omelet...

Creamed rice with pistachios and orange-flower water

Florence is a strange girl, who decided one day that from then on she would wear only soft stretchy clothes, to be sure of being comfortable, yet she still manages not to wear jogging suits. This is her favorite recipe "for good days," designed like her clothes to be simple and seamless. A bit old-fashioned, like rice pudding, with hints of pistachio and orange-flower water as a sign that there are other possibilities.

Preparation time: 40 minutes

· 1/4 cup (50 g) short-grain rice
· 1 1/4 cups (300 ml) milk
· 4 tsp superfine sugar
· 1 vanilla bean
· 1 egg yolk
· 1 tsp orange-flower water
· 1 tsp butter
· A few fresh pistachios

Bring a pan of salted water to a boil. Plunge the rice in it for 1 minute, then drain. Bring the milk to a boil, add the sugar, the vanilla, and finally the rice. Cook over a low heat for 30–35 minutes, stirring from

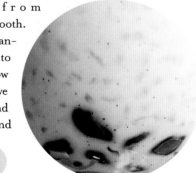

time to time to keep the consistency smooth. In a small bowl, mix the egg yolk and orange-flower water, then add this mixture to the contents of the pan and cook over low heat for an additional 1 minute. Remove from the heat, and mix in the butter and the pistachios. Pour into a serving dish and leave to cool.

Andean cream with mild spices

Have you tried living on cream and hope? It will ensure the final and lasting return, if not of your loved one, then at least of your equilibrium. Forget over-ambitious desserts for now, and those that are too sophisticated or contain too many calories. This one will blend in with the feeling of calm you get from your new suede slippers. Accompanied by green tea, could this be the happiness you've been looking for?

Preparation time: 30 minutes

· 1/3 cup (80 ml) + 1 1/2 tbsp milk
· 2 1/2 cups (600 ml) light cream
· 1/2 vanilla bean
· 2 pinches freshly grated nutmeg
· 1 cardamom pod
· 1/2 cinnamon stick
· 2 egg yolks
· 5 tsp superfine sugar

Preheat the oven to 350 °F (180 °C) and heat water for the bain-marie. Heat the milk and the cream with the vanilla (cut the bean open and scrape with the tip of a knife), nutmeg, cardamom seeds (contained in the pod, which you only have to open to get the seeds out), and the cinnamon stick. Remove from the heat and allow to infuse for a few minutes, then remove the vanilla bean and cinnamon stick and reserve. Keep very warm. In a bowl, beat the egg and sugar for 2 minutes, gradually mixing in the hot milk. The mixture should be smooth and creamy. Place the vanilla bean and the cinnamon stick in a ramekin, pour in the cream and put the ramekin in a baking dish filled with boiling water. Place in the oven and cook in the bain-marie for about 20 minutes. Allow to cool then place in the refrigerator for 2 hours before serving.

Strawberry and mango dessert with mint

Fancy something fresh without being forced to head for Hollywood or meet a femme fatale? Make this dessert your first step to salvation and go to the trouble of treating yourself to the recipes in the next chapter according to the mood—and the unpredictable nature—of the moment.

Preparation time: 7 minutes

- 2/3 cup (100 g) strawberries
- I mango
- I tbsp vanilla sugar
- 2 sprigs of mint

Wash the strawberries and cut in quarters. Peel the mango and cut the flesh in small pieces. Mix together in a bowl, and sprinkle with the vanilla sugar. Chop the mint leaves and add them to the fruit. Refrigerate for 30 minutes before serving.

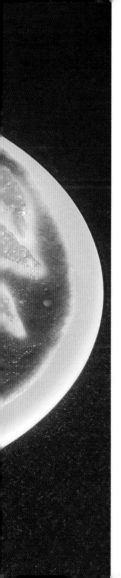

Fooling myself...
and his/her ghost as well

Hot, spicy, expensive recipes, too shameful to mention

Life's a bitch

Now you're back on track, with a fragile hope of enjoying plenty more little treats, but sometimes there are days when you've eaten all the chocolates, the boiler's broken down, and smiles have been replaced by blank looks. The days when the bosses are too busy, the customers are too fussy, and your colleagues are grinning all over but nobody deigns to tell you why. It's absolutely certain, they're all in

it together, it's a conspiracy. From the slice of bread that landed butter side down on your jeans to the guy who jostled you in the street, not to mention the friends who don't call you! You're the unluckiest person in the world. Even with your head under the pillow and your teeth clenched, you can't stop your lips trembling. "It's so unfair!"

Take a deep breath. Scream, if it will make you feel better, but scream as loud as you can and get rid of it! To stop yourself descending into a paranoid fear of being victimized that won't get you anywhere, put your burdensome past behind you as quickly as possible and be ready to bluff those around you… When you have the feeling that everything is happening to you and all the world is against you, you have to overcome it. It's up to you to defy fate, take things in hand, and abandon less important tasks.

When it comes to day-to-day essentials, go for what's simplest and, depending on how much spare cash you have, hire a cleaner and entrust her with your bucket and mops, and make a permanent arrangement with the local dry cleaners! But you can also transform these chores into times for play, or even sport, with the kind of music that will put you in a good mood and make you feel on top of the world again (try Marvin Gaye, The Jackson Five, Gloria Gaynor, or the irresistible "Twist 'n' Shout" by The Beatles)!

And if your career is stuck in a rut and your colleagues haven't changed for the last five years, who's stopping you from exploring the possibilities of getting a transfer, promotion, or even trying to retrain? The aim is to rise above events, while keeping your feet on the ground. That will give you the chance to make a few crazy plans, try something you've never dared to do, or invent new ways of doing everyday things. You can start by asking to have your purchases gift wrapped so you can have the fun of giving them to yourself, or by throwing out your ancient slippers and pajamas and deciding to walk around the house naked with the blinds down, or even by organizing sumptuous dinners just for you.

Every stage of this (re)construction is a gesture of defiance toward the fate we all believe we're victims of. You are regaining control of your life and are once again captain of the ship, and though it may have sprung a bit of a leak, you are sticking to your course. It's just a matter of time. Time to forget and time to reconquer the planet.

The aim of this chapter is to start the ship's engine again and be ready to steer clear of the obstacles along your course. You're alive, fine, but that isn't enough to stop you dying of boredom. The following recipes will lift your meals out of the routine, as though each day were a celebration.

Balm for the soul

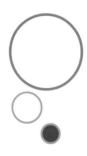

Perking up

Life as a couple had progressively
stifled your entrepreneurial spirit. It's time
to perk up and show yourself in a new light.
Start by buying yourself a fur coat, real or fake,
new or second-hand. Say, that's odd, the idea had
never even occurred to you before! Cozily wrapped inside this warm covering, you'll feel like
you're being held in your mom's arms or
hugged by a giant teddy bear. It's the
perfect comfort blanket.

Put yourself first

You don't have any guests this evening,
so invite yourself to dine like a prince or
princess: get out Granny's silverware, Aunt
Sophie's fine linen tablecloth, Grandpa's
candlesticks, and the scented candles. You've no
reason to envy VIPs or royalty. They're as
bored on their yachts as you would be on a
river boat… Let your ego blossom, even
while you're laughing at yourself.

The sea is in sight!

Jaws is on TV this evening, so why not treat yourself to a basket of oysters to savor while imagining your ex being eaten by sharks? Forget the events carefully marked on the calendar, leave the beaten track, and go off at a tangent. Yield to temptation, even on ordinary days (all the "non-anniversary" days), and while we're on the subject of pleasure, oysters are the winners in all categories: sexy, voluptuous, and an aphrodisiac—so they say.

Putting on the Ritz

Step inside a dress designer's for the first time: it's intoxicating. Wearing a new, slightly eccentric ensemble by Alexander McQueen will make you feel unique. If you're a bit hard up, wait for the sales or go for accessories (belts, scarves, hats, rings, key rings), or maybe very open shoes (there's not much of them, so they're less expensive!): Have you thought about flip-flops from Prada or Marc Jacobs?

It's all gone

You've changed your partner, then your apartment, sold your car, bought a season ticket for the subway, lost a few friends and forgotten to feed your goldfish, so they've died… Never mind, maybe it's the right moment to change your job as well and go and look elsewhere? What do you reckon?

Peppers with anchovies

You're still reeling from so many shocks that you don't know what waters you are swimming in or what height you're flying at. Come back down to earth but don't drown in the shallows! Turn your mind to the bell pepper, a vegetable firmly rooted in the soil, and the strong, sharp taste of anchovies in your mouth. Look at life alternately from the point of view of a farmer and a diver, and make the most of your formidable adaptability!

Preparation time: 30 minutes

· 3 whole salted anchovies (or 6 anchovy fillets)
· 2 small bell peppers of different colors
· 1/3 cup (75 ml) fruited olive oil
· Pepper

Rinse and fillet the whole anchovies, and carefully remove the large bones. Soak the anchovy fillets in cold water. Broil the peppers on each side until the skin blisters and blackens. Put them in a freezer bag (don't use any other kind of plastic bag, as some plastics contain poisonous chemicals). Meanwhile, heat the olive oil gently in a small pan. Drain, dry, and chop the anchovies, and put them in the pan with the oil. Stir this sauce frequently, taking care not to let it boil. Peel the peppers, remove the seeds, cut in quarters and dry. Arrange them on a plate and drizzle with the anchovy oil. Season with pepper.

Watercress soup with caviar

To enjoy this dish, you will have to not mind breaking open your piggy bank, otherwise forget it, or wait for a kindred spirit to offer you a chance to enjoy the taste of these expensive eggs, which always comes as a fresh surprise. Who cares if it's greedy—no more feelings of guilt and remorse! In Russia, being very rich means eating a can of caviar with two little spoons, one in each hand—that should put an end to your scruples! Having said that, you are rich, aren't you—apart from the money side of things?

Preparation time: 45 minutes

· I bunch of watercress
· 1/4 lb (100 g) potatoes
· I small onion
· I tbsp butter
· 1/2 cup (125 ml) milk
· I tbsp light cream
· Fresh herbs (choose from parsley, chives, tarragon, chervil, marjoram, and savory), finely chopped
· I heaping tsp caviar
· Salt and pepper

Wash, dry, and roughly chop the watercress. Wash and peel the potatoes, and cut into small cubes. Thinly slice the onion. Melt the butter gently in a pan, and add the onion, potatoes, and watercress. Allow to sweat for 5 minutes, without changing color. Pour over the milk and the same amount of water, bring to boiling point, then cook very gently for 30 minutes without allowing it to boil. Season lightly with salt and pepper. Process in a blender. Pour in a spiral of cream, sprinkle with chopped herbs and, using two small spoons, mold the caviar into an oval shape and place it delicately on top of the soup.

Baked egg with morels

Morels are rare and much sought after, so they are destined for you! They appear in spring from March to May, as soon as the snow thaws. However, it's better to buy them dried and vacuum-packed from the store than to rush out into the woods. It'll save you time and probably spare you the disappointment of not bumping into a friend or a lover. Woodcutters—if the word still conjures up in your mind the image of a strong, reassuring man—are an endangered species. As for the sex appeal of the woodcutter's wife…

Preparation time: 40 minutes

· Scant 1/4 oz (5 g) dried morels
· 2 tsp butter
· Lemon juice
· 1 egg, separated
· 1 tsp crème fraîche or sour cream
· Salt and pepper

Soak the morels in lukewarm water for 15 minutes, drain, then plunge into boiling water for 10 minutes. Rinse under running water and dry carefully. Preheat the oven to 415 °F (210 °C). Cut the biggest morels in two. Sauté them in a small skillet with the butter and a few drops of lemon juice. Butter a ramekin, and pour in the egg white. Season with salt and add the morels, arranging them in the shape of a little nest. Place the egg yolk and the crème fraîche or sour cream in the middle of the nest and season with pepper. Cover with aluminum foil and bake in the oven for 5 minutes.

Pan-fried green vegetables with sesame

Eating green vegetables is the start of a real health regime. Cooked together instead of separately, and transformed by ginger and sesame oil, they become as alluring as an invitation to meet the "most eligible bachelor of the year"… That's a secret our friend Ariane confided to us.

Preparation time: 20 minutes

· 10 oz (300 g) crisp green vegetables, combining equal weights of 3 different kinds (beans, asparagus, broccoli, bell peppers, sugar-snap peas, fennel, zucchini…)
· Oil for frying
· 1/2 inch (1 cm) piece of fresh gingerroot
· 1 garlic clove
· 1 tbsp sesame oil
· 1 tbsp sesame seeds
· Salt and pepper

Wash and trim all the vegetables, then cut them in pieces about 2 inches (5 cm) long. Heat a little oil in a skillet over high heat, and brown the mixture for about 10 minutes until the vegetables are golden on all sides. Reduce the heat and cover. Finely chop the ginger and the garlic clove and stir into the pan while the vegetables are still crisp. Add the sesame oil, season with salt and pepper, and replace the lid. At the same time, in another skillet, without any fat, brown the sesame seeds for barely a minute until they turn golden. Arrange the vegetables on a plate, and sprinkle with sesame seeds just before serving.

Egg with foie gras

Making something simple and delicious (sometimes) smacks of luxury, and that goes for this recipe. But you only have to explore your supermarket shelves to see that you can get small, relatively cheap cans of foie gras costing not much more than a jar of very fine jelly (a famous brand). If you're really broke, try plan B: swapping the foie gras for Gorgonzola cheese, whether Maï likes it or not (she gave us this pick-me-up recipe, which she makes any time she's feeling fragile). Whatever happens, adopt this motto: "Today, anything goes."

Preparation time: 15 minutes

· 1 tsp butter
· 3/4 oz (20 g) foie gras
· 1 tsp crème fraîche or sour cream
· 1 large, very fresh egg
· Salt and pepper

Heat 4 cups (1 liter) water. Preheat the oven to 350 °F (180 °C). Butter a fireproof ramekin. Put fine strips of foie gras in the bottom, and cover with the crème fraîche or sour cream. Break the egg into the ramekin without breaking the yolk. Salt lightly and pepper generously. Pour the boiling water into a small fireproof dish and place the ramekin in the middle. Put in the oven and cook for 10 minutes.

Variation

Instead of foie gras, cook the egg on a bed of crushed tomatoes with a little basil and Gorgonzola cheese.

Seafood lasagna

Need a good breath of fresh air, or a long voyage? In short, do you need to get away? A piece of advice: start by creating this story of sea spray and wide horizons in your kitchen, for a very reasonable price. Crab meat, peeled shrimp, a few scallops, and that's it: you're in Biarritz, Barcelona, Palermo, and you don't care what is happening back home. Still a bit stunned but eager and in love… just with life.

Preparation time: 45 minutes.

- 2 tsp butter
- 1 tbsp oil
- 1/4 lb (100 g) scallops
- 1 cup (200 g) sliced leeks
- 2 tbsp flat-leaf parsley
- Generous 1 cup (250 ml) light stock
- 1 pinch saffron
- 2 pinches piment d'Espelette or paprika
- 1 tbsp flour
- Scant 3 oz (80 g) peeled shrimp
- 2 crab claws, shelled
- 3 sheets of dry (ready-cook) lasagna
- 2 tbsp grated Parmesan cheese
- Pepper

Preheat the oven to 430 °F (220 °C). Heat the butter and oil in a large skillet. Sauté the scallops for 1 minute (no longer) on each side. Remove them with a slotted spoon and set aside. In the same oil, gently brown the leeks until tender. Meanwhile, chop the parsley and halve or quarter the biggest scallops. Heat the stock with the saffron and piment d'Espelette or paprika. Sprinkle the leeks with the flour and continue cooking for 2 minutes, stirring all the time. Gradually add the flavored stock while continuing to stir until the mixture thickens. Then add the scallops, shrimp, crab meat, and chopped parsley. Season with pepper, but do not add salt—there will be enough in the seafood and stock. In a rectangular dish the size of the lasagna sheets, arrange successive layers of a sheet of lasagna, a layer of filling, a little Parmesan, and so on, until all the ingredients have been used up, finishing with a layer of filling and a generous layer of

Parmesan. Bake in the oven for 20–25 minutes, until the surface is nice and golden.

Variation

The scallops may be replaced by mussels, clams, etc. All you need to do is cook them over high heat until they open and discard the shells. Reserve and strain the juices, and add sufficient stock to give 1 generous cup (250 ml) of liquid. Any kind of shellfish may be added to the recipe, according to your own taste.

Peach soup with vervain and pepper

This is the powerful elixir of youth, perfected by Sébastien, whose motto when cooking is "Always do everything as simply as possible while bringing out the flavors to the maximum." Your life may be under siege, but you still reign over the kingdom of your plate!

Preparation time: 15 minutes

· 2 very ripe yellow peaches
· 2 tbsp superfine sugar
· juice of 1/2 lemon
· 1 1/4 cups (300 ml) light, fruity red wine (the wine of Irany, near Chablis, is perfect)
· 2–3 leaves of fresh or dried vervain
· Pepper

Wash the peaches thoroughly, cut in quarters without removing the skins, and pour over the sugar and lemon juice. Heat the red wine for a good 10 minutes without letting it boil, to allow the alcohol to evaporate. Plunge the vervain leaves in it just before removing the pan from the heat. Then immerse the peaches in the flavored wine and allow to cool. Before serving, season with one twist of the pepper grinder.

Zabaglione with citrus fruits and rosemary

You're in a fragile state, and hurt by everything. You really feel the world is an awful place, and you've lost all sense of your body, because it's been numbed by the brutality around you. You don't even know if you're still capable of feeling pleasure. You need to be an island of serenity for this sophisticated dessert, which requires care, concentration, and dexterity. It'll be worth the effort, that's a promise, and the result is quite simply... amazing.

Preparation time: 35 minutes

· 1/2 white grapefruit
· 1/2 pink grapefruit
· 1 untreated orange
· 1 sprig of rosemary
· Grapefruit juice
· 2 egg yolks
· 1 tsp superfine sugar
· 1 tsp honey

Wash and dry the fruits and the rosemary. Cut a few thin strips of orange peel, then remove the peel and pith from the fruits, and separate into segments, taking care to reserve the juice. Dry the segments on paper towels and arrange them on a heatproof plate. Add grapefruit juice to the juice from the fruit to make 3 1/2 tablespoons. Warm this juice in a small pan with the rosemary, but do not allow to boil. Turn off the heat and allow to infuse for 10 minutes (no longer, the aroma is very strong). Preheat the broiler. In a pan, heat water for the bain-marie to simmering point. In a bowl that will fit in the pan, beat the egg yolks and the sugar for 2 minutes to make a pale, frothy mixture. Pour in the honey and the infusion, while whipping to a light cream. Place the bowl in the pan and beat the zabaglione for 5 minutes until it swells and thickens. Pour the hot zabaglione over the fruits and broil for 1–2 minutes to give it a light golden crust. Decorate with the reserved strips of peel and serve very quickly.

Carpaccio of pineapple with olive oil

Astonishing as this association of a fruit, an oil, and a spice may seem, they are in perfect harmony. The dream has become a dessert. Choose a very ripe pineapple, because its juice will suddenly be filled with sunshine when it meets the olive oil. Your tropical paradise may be quite close, without your having to go to Tahiti. Head south...

Preparation time: 10 minutes

· 1/2 pineapple, very ripe
· 1 vanilla bean
· Sweet olive oil

Cut off half the pineapple and remove the skin. Divide the fruit in thin slices and arrange on a plate. Drizzle lightly with olive oil, choosing a very sweet one (Nyons olive oil is wonderful), and sprinkle with fresh vanilla seeds, obtained by cutting the bean in half lengthwise and scraping out the seeds with a knife.

Spiced date pastilla

You're half way across the desert and the camel has kicked the bucket. You know all about cold, lonely nights, but here is a sweet treat full of contrasts with a soft heart and a crisp coating, and a hint of the exotic to enliven your boredom. Now you can open your eyes to the beauties of the starry skies, the charm of mint tea at overnight camps, the opportunities of oases... isn't that right, habibi?

Preparation time: 35 minutes

· 6 dried dates
· 1/2 untreated lemon
· 1 tbsp brown rum
· 2 pinches grated nutmeg
· 1 clove
· 6 unsalted toasted pistachios
· 1 tsp butter
· 2 sheets brick (thin Tunisian pastry) or phyllo pastry
· A few caraway seeds
· Ground cinnamon

Preheat the oven to 345 °F (175 °C). Pit the dates and cut in small pieces. Wash the lemon half, cut in rounds, and remove the seeds. In a small pan, heat 1 generous cup (250 ml) water with the rum, nutmeg, clove, and lemon slices. When the mixture comes to a boil, add the dates and pistachios. Simmer for 10 minutes, remove from the heat and allow to cool. Meanwhile, melt the butter. Lightly brush one side of the sheets of pastry and arrange them butter side down on the work surface. Strain the syrup and put the fruits (except the lemon) in the middle of one sheet of pastry. Fold over the four sides and place folds down on top of the other sheet of pastry. Fold the second sheet in the same way and place folds down on a baking sheet. Brush with melted butter and sprinkle with caraway seeds. Bake in the oven for 15 minutes. While it is baking, chop the lemon slices and return them to the syrup. Reduce the syrup until the lemon pith becomes translucent. Serve the pastilla with a dash of syrup and a pinch of cinnamon and nutmeg.

Taking it out on food

Desperate situations call for desperate measures!

Stuff the lot of them!

Having got back into the swing of things, you want to do it all, see it all, drink everything that's going. The time for regrets is past. After all, it has been a bit like casting your pearls before swine, hasn't it? So now it's time to leave this barnyard life to a new candidate for the happy farm. You were just expecting too much, chomping at the bit, hoping in vain that the other person would jump, and in the end you were trying too hard in order to make up for their lack of enthusiasm. Since then, you've been eating for two, stuffing down his/her share as well as yours. You never stop, you go out all the time, work on projects and, because you're more active than ever, you've convinced yourself that everything's fine. But have you ever asked yourself whether you're really happy? All these activities that are eating into your sleep-time are beginning to make you irritable, and this frantic rush has the same numbing effect on you as the initial shock.

While you're in this phase of trying to ease your frustration, you're a bit like a quack advertising his ancient magic potion for getting rid of the blues. Set yourself simple targets, like going for a walk without having shopping to do or friends to go and see. How long is it since you last left home with no special aim in mind, went on a crazy window-shopping spree, or just sat and looked at the flowers? Rediscover the

pleasure of being yourself, moving at your own pace. And why not throw a party just for yourself from time to time? Cook yourself a little meal, and if it has to simmer for a while, maybe immerse yourself in a good book. It's all about escaping without leaving your couch, or if you're afraid of being bored, why not commune with a cat, or even call some old friends. Enjoy eating a homemade dessert. Mmm! Then slide under the quilt and sleep!

My, it's a long time since you had time for a proper breakfast, so eat it slowly and use the time to think about the next dish that will make your engine start first time, because food is life. Make sure you choose good food, so you don't run entirely on carbs or sink into the sort of orgiastic delirium seen in Marco Ferreri's movie La Grande Bouffe.

Now the engine is running again, this stage is concerned with not letting it break down through overheating. Rediscover the virtue of patience, make long, careful preparations and really take time to cook. The recipes in this chapter are nourishing, substantial, and sometimes take quite a long time to prepare, but the rewards are all the greater!

A few words of advice on getting back on your feet

Do you remember the effect of the banquet in Babette's Feast? Stéphane Audran, leaning over her stove, demonstrating that pleasure begins with food, to bring a little joy into the lives of an austere and loveless community. Start by going out to look for some nice china so you will be ready for all eventualities. It's a good excuse for discovering one or two original designers!

Make the kitchen a creative area

If you're going to reinvent your life, the kitchen is an ideal place for all kinds of experiments. If you want to force the hand of fate, yield to the temptation of treating yourself to some new equipment: an ice cream maker, waffle machine, pasta maker, sandwich toaster, mandolin, melon baller, fish kettle, conical strainer, wok, pastry bag...

Gloubiboulga

There was a character in the French version of Sesame Street who every night would wolf down a mixture called gloubiboulga, and we all wondered what it was made of. It's up to you to invent your own hyperenergizing miracle recipe to get you out of the dumps and make you forget that idiot (the one who left you or the one you left—not the TV character). It's not the right time for slimming diets that will make you wan and depressed—it's more a time for excess. If you want to go far, take care of your horse and drink your gloubi!

Ever increasing

Once upon a time the choice at the gas station was premium or regular. It's much the same in your kitchen. It's up to you to choose. The "high octane" diet cannot be too highly recommended—not necessarily in terms of quantity, but for quality, we'd have no hesitation!

Camomile

If you can't stop eating, consider herbal teas to get you back on your feet. Roman camomile has a soothing effect on the digestion. It's more effective than medicines, and is also recommended after drinking bouts. Why not try a camomile tea right now?

Pasta with herbs

This is as easy and comforting as a bowl of cornflakes, but a great deal better as an antidepressant, because the mixture of fresh aromatic herbs gives it an unusual flavor with reviving qualities. Something to perk you up and leave your feet on the ground but your head still in the clouds.

Preparation time: 15 minutes

· 7 cherry tomatoes
· 4 basil leaves
· 3 sprigs of flat-leaf parsley
· 2 sprigs of chervil
· 1 pinch dried marjoram flowers
· 1 garlic clove
· 2 tbsp olive oil
· Vegetable stock
· 1/4 lb (125 g) pasta

Wash and dry the cherry tomatoes and the herbs. Chop the herbs. Peel the garlic and chop fine. Heat the olive oil in a skillet and gently brown the cherry tomatoes and garlic for 10 minutes. Add a little vegetable stock as necessary to prevent the garlic burning and turning bitter. Meanwhile, cook the pasta in plenty of boiling salted water with a drop of olive oil. Drain the pasta and add to the pan, along with the chopped herbs. Mix and serve.

Waterzoi (fish soup)

You aren't lucky enough to have a log fire to warm your aching heart? Consider waterzoi, a Belgian specialty with a hint of beer that goes well with the fish and will set you up nicely.

Preparation time: 35 minutes

- I carrot
- 2 potatoes
- I leek
- I/2 onion
- Butter
- I/2 bouillon cube
- 2/3 cup (150 ml) beer
- I bay leaf
- I sprig of thyme
- I salmon steak
- I small cod fillet
- I tbsp crème fraîche or sour cream
- I egg yolk
- Salt and pepper

Wash the carrot, potatoes, and leek, then chop in small pieces together with the onion half. Brown the chopped vegetables in a large saucepan with a little butter for 3–4 minutes. At the same time, bring I 2/3 cups (400 ml) water to a boil and dissolve the half bouillon cube in it. Pour this stock and the beer into the pan with the vegetables. Season with salt and pepper, and add the bay leaf and thyme. Cover and cook for 15 minutes, stirring occasionally. Add the two pieces of fish and continue cooking for 5 minutes. When the fish is cooked, remove the pan from the heat, add the crème fraîche or sour cream and the egg yolk and stir. Eat as a soup or with rice as a main dish.

Normandy tartiflette

You've given your stomach such a hard time it's complaining, and your indifference is driving it to despair… So get going, confront the ogre sleeping inside you, before you collapse! Have you decided to devote your life to novelty from now on? Try this revamped version of the traditional tartiflette, which uses Pont l'Évêque instead of Reblochon cheese and cider instead of white wine… Don't even think about starving to death for love—what a waste! There's so much ahead of you that you'd do better to prepare your stomach for endurance. It's all about being ready for the best—and nothing but the best, this time.

Preparation time: 35 minutes

· 3 potatoes
· 3 scallions
· Butter
· 2 oz (50 g) bacon, diced
· 3 tbsp hard cider
· 1/2 Pont l'Évêque cheese
    (about 6 oz/ 175 g)

Peel the potatoes, cut in half, and steam for about 10 minutes. Preheat the oven to 465 °F (240 °C). Peel the scallions, slice thinly, then brown in a skillet with a little butter. Blanch the bacon by plunging it in a pan of boiling water for 2–3 minutes to take away some of the fat. Place the potatoes in a gratin dish with the scallions and bacon, then pour over the cider. Cover with slices of cheese, cut horizontally. Bake in the oven for about 20–25 minutes.

Morteau sausage with Cancoillotte cheese

To combat starvation try this typically fortifying dish from Franche-Comté. It's quick and easy, and will make you feel you'll soon be tying up in harbor, instead of being tossed between the devil and the deep blue sea, as on those stormy days when your whole world seems to be collapsing. Stiffen your morale with a coating of Cancoillotte; you'll feel all the better for it.

Preparation time: 30 minutes

· 1 small Morteau sausage (or other French spiced sausage)
· 3 or 4 small potatoes
· 1 small carton of natural Cancoillotte (or cream cheese)
· A few lettuce leaves
· A few juniper berries

Place the sausage (without pricking it, in order to retain all the spices) in a pan of cold water. Bring to a boil and simmer for 20 minutes. Meanwhile, wash and peel the potatoes and steam for 15–20 minutes. Melt the Cancoillotte in a bain-marie or put it in the microwave for a few seconds. Arrange the potatoes and sausage on the lettuce leaves and pour the melted Cancoillotte over. Garnish with a few juniper berries.

Penne with nettles

The black comedy version: you could cheerfully have chucked your ex into a patch of nettles, so enjoy this dish while imagining this basic comic movie scene, which will have you in a laughing fit. The happy version: enjoy this pasta, and this time laugh out loud at the thought of our friend Gianni, the creator of this recipe, who had such a high opinion of his prowess with women that he'd take them for a roll in the nettles rather than the hay… Quite apart from the effects of this story, the fresh nettles brighten up the penne by adding a subtle hint of nutmeg, and the warmth of the pasta is enough to prevent them from stinging your mouth.

Preparation time: 15 minutes

· 1/4 lb (100 g) penne
· 1/2 cup (25 g) fresh nettles
· Crème fraîche or sour cream
· Parmesan cheese, grated
· Salt

Cook the penne according to the instructions on the package. Meanwhile, chop the nettles finely (using a knife, not a food processor), taking care to handle them on the backs so they don't sting. Drain the pasta. Season with salt, add a little crème fraiche or sour cream and grated Parmesan, then stir in the raw nettles.

Variation

This recipe also works perfectly using ricotta cheese in place of the crème fraîche.

Neeps and tatties

This is famous as the traditional accompaniment to the Scottish haggis—sheep's stomach stuffed with seasoned ground meat—but it can also be eaten on its own. As well as fortifying you, it's also a perfect way to express your current state of mind: still appetizing, even when alone.

Preparation time: 30 minutes

- 3 boiling potatoes
- 2 turnips
- 3–4 shallots
- Olive oil
- 2/3 cup (150 ml) milk
- Salt and pepper

Peel the potatoes and turnips and cut in pieces. Place them in a pan of boiling salted water and cook for about 20 minutes. Meanwhile, slice the shallots thinly and brown in a skillet in a little olive oil until golden. Set aside. Heat the milk in a large pan. Drain the potatoes and turnips, plunge them in the hot milk, then mash roughly with a fork. Season with salt and pepper, and add the warm shallots and a dash of olive oil.

Apple cake

Jean-Christophe is a friend. For a long time he was the iconic bachelor. Then along came Anne, a whirlwind of smiles, words, and ideas. Jean-Christophe kidnapped this generous and amusing person, and carried her off to live at the other end of the world... She just had enough time to leave us a family recipe that is exactly like her: simple, generous, and unmistakable!

Preparation time: 20 minutes

- 3 tbsp butter
- 2 tbsp superfine sugar
- 1 egg
- Scant 1/2 cup (50 g) all-purpose flour
- 1/2 tsp baking powder
- 2 pinches ground cinnamon
- 1 pinch salt
- 1 dessert apple, sliced

Preheat the oven to 350 °F (180 °C). Melt the butter in a pan over low heat. Remove from the heat and stir in the sugar. Continue stirring until the sugar has completely dissolved. Add the egg, flour, baking powder, cinnamon, and salt and stir until smooth. In a small round dish like a charlotte mold, place half the apple slices, pour over the flour mixture, and arrange the remaining apple slices on top. Bake in the oven for 15 minutes. Best eaten hot or warm.

Yvonne's pain délice

Why not try combining two well-known desserts: tarte Tatin and honeycake, which in this recipe goes very well with a topping of caramelized pears? It's a matter of nerve, and also a way of paying homage to the bonds that stretch back over time through recipes handed down from generation to generation, because the honeycake recipe comes from my much-loved grandmother, who would have considered this hybrid weird but cheeky.

Preparation time: 1 hour 15 minutes

- 7 lumps of white sugar
- 1 very ripe pear
- 2/3 cup (150 ml) milk
- Scant 1 1/2 cups (250 g) whole wheat flour
- 1/2 cup (150 g) honey
- Scant 1/2 cup (100 g) superfine sugar
- 1 tsp baking soda
- 1 tsp aniseed

Preheat the oven to 300 °F (150 °C). In a Tatin mold or heatproof cake pan, heat the sugar lumps with 2 tablespoons water to form a caramel. Do not stir with a spoon, you only need to wait for the sugar to change color. When it is brown, remove the pan from the heat. Peel the pear, cut in quarters, and arrange on the caramel. Heat the milk. Mix together the flour, honey, and superfine sugar and blend in the hot milk to give a thick smooth dough. Add the baking soda and the aniseed, then pour the mixture into the mold, over the pears. Bake in the oven for 1 hour. Check whether the cake is cooked inside by inserting a knife in it. Turn out of the mold so the fruit is on top and serve warm or cold. This dessert keeps very well for several days and is even better the next day… if there's any left.

Oatmeal with chestnuts

If your heart needs to be filled with something down-to-earth and healthy, this wonderful porridge with chestnut puree will put you on the right track. Oats and milk are the perfect image of dependable comfort food, like a couple who have stuck together for a long time. Without wallowing in nostalgia, take a few seconds to succumb to this idea...

Preparation time: 5 minutes

· 5 tbsp rolled oats
· 1/3 cup (80 ml) milk
· 2 tbsp superfine sugar
· Finely grated zest of 1/2 orange
· 5 whole almonds
· 4 hazelnuts
· 1 tsp chestnut puree

Heat the rolled oats and milk together in a saucepan, then add the sugar, orange zest, and the whole almonds and hazelnuts. Cook for a few minutes, stirring occasionally until you get the desired consistency. Pour into a deep plate and spoon over the chestnut puree.

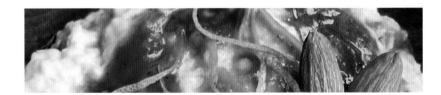

Variation

The chestnut puree may be replaced by jelly, which will liven up the porridge in the same way.

Pain perdu with prunes in Armagnac

To banish the pangs of love that have turned you to marshmallow, here is a feisty dessert that will get you back on your feet and fill you with joy. The hint of Armagnac will put you in a romantic frame of mind, like one of the Three Musketeers, ready to fight for love and honor. Don't forget, humor can rescue you from anything, especially love.

Preparation time: 40 minutes

- 3 or 4 ready-to-eat prunes
- 2 tsp Armagnac
- 1 egg
- 1 tbsp superfine sugar
- 1 tbsp crème fraîche or sour cream
- Generous cup (250 ml) milk
- 1/2 tbsp vanilla sugar
- 2 slices of bread
- Brown sugar

Split the prunes in half and soak in the Armagnac for 15 minutes. Preheat the oven to 350 °F (180 °C). Heat the milk in a pan with the vanilla sugar, then allow to cool. In a bowl, mix the egg, sugar, and crème fraîche. Soak the bread slices in the cooled sweetened milk. Butter a cake pan or ovenproof dish, choosing a narrow shape so that the slices of bread are firmly wedged and the creamy mixture cannot expand too far sideways. Lift the bread from the milk and pile in the bottom of the dish. Combine the vanilla milk and the egg mixture and pour over the bread. Sprinkle with brown sugar and bake for 30 minutes. Serve warm with the prunes.

Marriages that last

The ones that will never let you down!

Love stories end in tears

Well, here we are. You're not feeling too bad now, but you're still a bit off-color. Something may have been destroyed, like your illusions. It wouldn't surprise you. You don't believe in them any more. All the fairy stories, all the solemn promises like "to love and to cherish till death do us part" pledged with a honeyed "I do" and accompanied by a self-satisfied smile, and all the other silly nonsense—it all seems so stupid that it takes an effort of the imagination to remind yourself that you were in it up to the neck. And not so long ago, either! Love stories, thank you very much, you've done your bit. What you have learned is that there's no point putting your money on a horse: good or bad, they all run in one direction, and it isn't toward you.

In short, totally disillusioned, even disenchanted, you have decided to let cold, implacable, objective observation rule your life. Brrr! But stop reading depressing philosophical literature for a minute! If you are studying the couple and its inevitable demise, you should also study those that endure. Surely you must have some friends who have lived together a good few years (even if you've been carefully avoiding them recently)? You may argue that they're not old enough to be

conclusive examples, but all the same, you may be aware of little elderly couples among your acquaintances, who've been married forever and are still firmly attached to one another. And it's not always just habit, a good pension, or Viagra that keeps them together! You admit you find them touching, and your newly acquired heart of stone is close to melting.

You wouldn't have fallen so far, if you hadn't had such high hopes, and maybe when you obstinately assert your new convictions, you're repudiating your own old opinions. And all so as not to get involved and to be sure of not being hurt again. It's a sign of weakness, and a good sign—for the same reason—of your capacity for love. A love that's still fearful of getting involved. But you haven't got as far as that yet, you're only looking for adventure with a very small "a"—just a frisson or a spark of romance— and you're keeping your fragile little heart warm. It's had a rough time. Meanwhile, a few sessions of watching great love stories with tragic endings will make you cry a little, and you'll be grateful to get back to the ones that end happily!

This stage is important, because it's about reminding yourself that a battle is not a war, that setbacks can be turned into successes, and that obstacles sometimes make good stepping stones. Here is a series of recipes that prove that lasting values still exist and always will.

One day my prince will come...

Cooking from the pantry

As you have probably noticed, the refrigerator of someone newly single often resembles his/her life—half empty. So much the better; it's good practice for positive thinking! Ban all sighs, regrets, and reproaches, and invent your own little dish using those few leftovers. Isn't your latest challenge to learn to make do with what is there (instead of what isn't there anymore)?

The condemned woman

Do you remember that "condemned woman" in David Lynch's Twin Peaks? She seemed to have no other purpose than to make her presence felt, regardless of the passage of time. Suppose you model yourself on her? As you cross the desert, try to make good use of this in-between time, with no real aim other than to confirm your place among the human race. That would be a good start.

Joke

The shortest jokes are often the best, so why shouldn't the same go for love stories?

92

Destiny

This story started as a fairytale and it's ending like a bad TV soap. It's enough to put you off your food. Why not revisit the books or movies that have made your heart beat faster, with legendary couples like Anthony and Cleopatra, Tristan and Isolde, Humphrey Bogart and Lauren Bacall. It's all about distancing yourself from your own story with its unsatisfactory plot.

Proverbs

Spend a whole day trying to call to mind a series of (real or invented) proverbs to make yourself feel you're in an enviable situation: "Win some, lose some," "You can't do the impossible," "Too many cooks spoil the broth," "The road to hell is paved with good intentions."… You're feeling better already, aren't you?

Golden wedding

So your grandparents made it to their golden wedding and your parents are well on the way to doing the same? OK. But aside from being amazingly enduring, married life is not a competition. That might offer you some consolation today.

Cheese & wine

Looking for the quickest and easiest way to give yourself pleasure? Select a cheese and the best wine to go with it. They're like a couple who amaze you by always doing everything together, with a marriage that's as firm and secure as the perfect blend of eggs and oil in mayonnaise. Except that mayonnaise will sometimes curdle. On the other hand, opting for the marriage of wine and cheese is a way of limiting the risks and it's a relationship that's sure to last to the very end of your life! Here are some combinations we recommend you to try (with your eyes shut) if you get the chance.

· Creamy Chaource goes amazingly well with white Burgundy and a few fresh hazelnuts.

· All goat cheeses will be enhanced by a Sancerre, a dash of honey, and a few toasted almonds.

· An unpasteurized Camembert will reveal its full flavor with an Anjou wine.

· The strength and density of Beaufort demands a white Artois.

· Roquefort and Sauternes is a marriage made in heaven.

· A sheep's cheese is a perfect match for a dry Vouvray, and a little red currant jelly makes a good accompaniment.

Mini sandwiches & Bloody Mary

Are you really hungry, yet still only wanting to nibble at food, so as not to lose
your new sparrow-like eating habits? To avoid dragging an ugly, leaking sandwich (or one that will certainly leak its contents) into the living room, why not
make it in bite-size pieces, so you can hold a glass of something restorative and
nourishing in your other hand to sip while you relax?

For the sandwiches

· I large tomato
· 6 slices of sandwich bread
· Curd cheese or lowfat cream
  cheese
· Prepared mustard
· 4 large lettuce leaves
· 2 slices of cheese
· 2 slices of ham
· Salt and pepper

For the Bloody Mary

· 2 ice cubes
· 1/4 glass vodka
· 3/4 glass tomato juice
· I squeeze lemon juice
· A few drops of Worcestershire sauce
· Tabasco
· Celery salt

Preparation time: 10 minutes

Slice the tomato. Toast the slices of bread. Spread four slices with cream cheese and
season with salt and pepper.
Spread mustard on both
sides of the remaining two
slices. Assemble a sandwich: on
a slice spread with cheese place two
lettuce leaves, a slice of cheese, a half
slice of crumpled ham, a slice spread
with mustard, another half slice of
ham, slices of tomato, and a second
slice spread with cheese. Stick
4 toothpicks through the sandwich,
cut off the crusts and cut in four.
Make a second sandwich in the same
way. Pour all the ingredients for the
cocktail into a big glass, mix, and
drink.

Bruschetta with pesto & Lambrusco

A real delicacy to make just for yourself, so you can lick your fingers without feeling at all embarrassed, because that would obviously spoil the pleasure... Making this pesto yourself means it will have a stronger flavor and a less oily texture than the mass-produced variety. The combination of homemade pesto and Lambrusco Secco, a sparkling and unpretentious dry Italian red wine, will delight you without getting you too drunk (about 10.5% proof).

Preparation time: 15 minutes

· 10 thin slices French bread or ciabatta
· 2 tbsp pine nuts
· 2 tbsp grated Parmesan cheese
· 3 tbsp chopped basil
· 1 garlic clove
· 1 tbsp olive oil
· 10 sun-dried tomatoes in oil
· 10 Parmesan shavings

Toast one side of the slices of bread for 2 minutes under the broiler. Process the pine nuts, grated Parmesan, basil, garlic, and olive oil in a blender. Spread this pesto on each slice of bread, place a tomato and a shaving of Parmesan on top. Nibble with a glass of Lambrusco Secco. Mmm!... happiness at last!

Chicken with chutney & piña colada

I remember an unforgettable conversation overheard on a train between Mumbai and Kochi in India: "Of course marriages are arranged. Love is only for the cinema!" And does it work by proxy? Well it's time to plunge into the world of Bollywood, to take a course of treatment by love story, where fluttering eyelids and kitsch choreography provide consolation for being alone in bed… With a meal on a tray, directly inspired by that part of the world.

For the chicken rolls

· 7 oz (200 g) boneless chicken breast
· 2 thin slices of jambon cru or prosciutto
· About 1/3 cup (100 g) hot spiced chutney
· 2 tsp butter
· Lettuce leaves

For the piña colada

· 2 ice cubes
· 2/10 glass white rum
· 1/10 glass coconut milk
· 1/10 glass light cream
· 6/10 glass pineapple juice

Preparation time: 20 minutes

Preheat the oven to 350 °F (180 °C). Cut the chicken breast lengthwise into two thin slices. Place a slice of ham on each and spread with some of the chutney. Roll up and fix with a toothpick. Melt the butter in a small saucepan with 1 teaspoon chutney and brush the rolls with it. Place the chicken rolls on a baking sheet and cook in the oven for 15 minutes, basting with chutney halfway through cooking. While they are cooking, pour all the ingredients for the cocktail into a shaker and shake vigorously (the pineapple juice will foam!). Pour into a large glass and drink well chilled with the hot chicken rolls and a few lettuce leaves.

Canapés & mojito

It's time to repossess your space and relax on the sofa with a book. To celebrate this event, we have a little tray of light, refreshing appetizers, extremely classy, but made from almost nothing.

For the canapés

· 1 cucumber
· 1 small can tuna
· 1 tbsp fromage frais or plain yogurt
· 2 tbsp prepared mustard
· 1 tsp lemon juice
· 6 black olives, chopped
· 1 tbsp chopped chives
· 1/2 red bell pepper, cored, seeded, and chopped
· 1 tbsp chopped parsley
· Salt

For the mojito

· 5–7 fresh mint leaves
· 1 tsp superfine sugar
· 2 dashes lemon juice
· Crushed ice
· 3/4 glass white rum

Preparation time: 10 minutes

Slice the cucumber in rounds 3/8 inch (1/2) cm thick. Sprinkle with salt, allow to stand for 15 minutes, then rinse, and dry thoroughly. In a bowl, mix the drained tuna, fromage frais or yogurt, mustard, and lemon juice. Divide this mixture in half and put in two separate bowls. Stir the chopped black olives and chives into one half, and the chopped bell pepper and parsley into the other. Place a dollop of mixture on each slice of cucumber. In a thick glass and using a pestle, crush the mint leaves together with the sugar and lemon juice. Half fill the glass with crushed ice and add the rum.

Munster cheese pastry & a glass of beer

Something that's "as easy as pie" immediately finds its opposite in "too hard, I give up." No, life is definitely not and never will be a tranquil stream; it's more like a path strewn with obstacles, and with many branches leading off it. So sip your beer and hope, like your childhood hero Starsky (unless it was MacGyver), to negotiate the next bend safely. This is your short-term objective...

Preparation time: 15 minutes

- 1 sheet of ready-rolled puff pastry
- 1 Munster cheese (about 10 oz/300 g)
- A few caraway seeds
- 1 egg yolk, beaten
- 1 beer

Preheat the oven to 430 °F (220 °C). Lay the pastry on a flan dish, and cut in half. Cut the Munster horizontally, to give two rounds of cheese. Put one round on each half of the pastry, and sprinkle with caraway seeds. Fold the pastry over the cheese to make turnovers. Press the edges down well and brush with a little beaten egg yolk. Bake in the oven for a good 10 minutes and eat with a cold beer.

Sardines tartare & Campari-grapefruit

This is the aperitif for happy days, to rouse you from the lethargy that frankly isn't getting you anywhere. TV commercials for candy bars have a great way of suggesting that their product will get you going. The placebo effect? Tell yourself that Campari and grapefruit and these mouthfuls of sardine on toast will have the same effect on you!

For the tartare
· 1 can sardines in olive oil
· Juice of 1/2 lemon
· 2 tsp crème fraîche or sour cream
· 1 tsp Dijon mustard
· Parsley
· Salt and pepper
· Toast

For the cocktail
· 1/3 glass Campari
· 2/3 glass grapefruit juice
· Ice cubes

Preparation time: 10 minutes

Remove the backbones from the sardines and roughly chop the fish. In a bowl, mix the lemon juice, crème fraîche or sour cream and mustard. Add the chopped sardines and mix. Chop and stir in the parsley. Season with salt and pepper. Pour the ingredients for the cocktail into a big glass, mix, and drink well chilled. Serve with toast.

Variation
The grapefruit juice may be replaced with orange juice, though grapefruit juice is our unconditional favorite.

Samosas & an infusion of ginger

Cutting down your cooking to individual proportions isn't that easy, especially if your appetite is also at half-mast. So it's highly likely you've started to build up a collection of leftovers. But don't wait until they've turned green before getting them out of the refrigerator... No, there are other alternatives, including this recipe. Accompanied by this powerful drink (no alcohol, it's OK!), these samosas will enable you to recycle your old bits and pieces into a delicious meal.

For the samosas

· 1/2 onion, chopped
· 4–5 oz (125 g) ground meat
· 1 garlic clove, crushed
· 2 tbsp tomato sauce
· 5 sheets brick (thin Tunisian pastry) or phyllo pastry
· 1 tbs melted butter
· Lettuce leaves

For 4 cups (1 liter) of infusion

· 5 inch (12.5 cm) piece of fresh gingerroot
· 2 cloves
· Lemon juice

Preparation time: 20 minutes + cooling time

To prepare the infusion in advance, peel the ginger, grate or process in a blender, place in a saucepan and cover with 4 cups (1 liter) cold water. Add 2 cloves and bring to a boil. Simmer over low heat for 10 minutes. Remove from the heat, add a few drops of lemon juice and allow to infuse until completely cold. Strain and keep cool. For the samosas, preheat the oven to 345 °F (175 °C.) Sauté the onion, meat, and garlic, then add the tomato sauce. Cut the sheets of pastry into strips about 3 inches (8 cm) wide. Put a portion of meat filling on a strip, fold it into a triangle and brush with melted butter. Proceed in the same way with the rest of the filling. Cook the samosas on a baking sheet in the oven for 12 minutes. Serve with a few lettuce leaves and the chilled infusion.

Variation
The ingredients for the filling may be replaced by leftovers of cheese, dishes in sauce, garnishes, cooked meat, etc.

I'm turning into someone else

Poisonous pleasures

Champagne!

Nothing is more inhibiting than the sober image people have of you. After all this time you've had enough of your friends' solicitous looks, the comforting hands on your shoulder, and those faces with calm smiles and wrinkled brows asking, "Well, how are things with you?" And either you reply resolutely, "Absolutely great!" (and they tell themselves that you're exaggerating) or you say soberly, "Fine. How about you?" (and then they reckon you're covering up). It's infuriating, and you just want to be left in peace and see people who didn't know you when you were with your ex.

It's time to shuffle the cards. You are in charge of the game and you decide to play your best card. In this phase you put yourself to the test as a challenge, throwing down the gauntlet to life, instead of throwing a bottle into the sea.

Even your own perception of yourself is confining. You've been feeling restricted and uncomfortable, as though you were wearing a very old suit. Looking at the big picture and seeing things in a different way will finally release you from this evil spell. Changing your hairstyle, your glasses, or any accessory that forms part of

 your identity in other people's eyes could trigger a change in your outlook on the world and vice versa.

Brazenly, you decide that anything goes, and invent romantic situations, like sending yourself flowers at the office (yes, especially you, gentlemen), just to set the tongues wagging, or spread the word about the notorious chocolate orgasm (yes, it really does exist, see page 132). That way you'll start to sow the seeds of doubt.

Write your own story, full of thrills and suspense, and bring a little glamor into your life. Make yourself out to be irresistible and sparkle like champagne, terrifying the mouse that unexpectedly falls into your clutches. And finally, issue an invitation to the acquaintance who has been eyeing you fondly for months without either of you making up your mind to

start a private conversation, even if it only involves spending a delightful evening talking about this and that with someone who is interested in the subject... Of course it's understood that you are not the center of the universe (at least, not yet), but Destiny awaits you at the corner of the street, and there are a thousand and one ways of triggering it into action.

In this chapter, we suggest you widen your range of opportunities. The fact that you are trying to recover your morale doesn't mean you're obliged to rebuild your old self. All the recipes in this chapter are sinful, spicy, or alcoholic. It's all about livening up the everyday routine.

You're in charge!

Making your life a work of art

Suppose you were to decide not to go traveling and to buy a work of art instead? Art is a much better idea! Remember Robert Filliou's words of wisdom, "Art is what makes life more interesting than art."

All the first times

The end of a story is always a bit staggering, but how liberating as well. Be brave enough to do all the things you haven't yet done that fall into the category of "permissible sins," like dinner with champagne, smoking cigars, getting a tattoo, starting to learn about wine, taking up singing or kick boxing... Go places where you aren't expected. You have nothing to lose and everything to gain.

Health = beauty

You're still not feeling quite yourself, but you sense that you soon could be again. Chairman Mao is supposed to have recommended that you rely on your own strengths... What are your resources? They are inside you, and will awaken as soon as you have your heart set on developing them—a new hair color, a bath oil, a new shampoo you've never tried, a sauna in the middle of winter, a facial at the beauty parlor. Do it for yourself first, and then for others.

114

Strength of belief

You don't have the means to satisfy your new passions and desires? It's the perfect time to ask your boss for a raise, to reinforce your image as an out-and-out winner. Who dares wins, so make that your motto.

Casino

Suppose you give fate a bit of a nudge, instead of moaning about how your life keeps going off track? Go and gamble 75 dollars in an evening at the casino, and you'll see which way the wind is blowing. Heads or tails, red or black, abandon yourself entirely to chance.

Sea or mountains, why choose?

"If you don't like the sea, if you don't like the mountains, if you don't like the country, then go to hell!" said Jean-Paul Belmondo in the Godard movie Breathless... If you think hard about it, what do you really like? Suppose you were to try something different? The Andes and Méribel, the Ile de Sein and the Maldives, la Creuse and the Ukraine, Morocco and Cuba ? Give the globe a spin, play a game of chance by stopping it at some country with your finger, and launch yourself into the adventure of unknown territory.

Shrimp with whiskey

You can work wonders in the kitchen without getting out the big guns, and achieve miraculous results like this happy combination of alcohol with some pretty young creatures from the sea. Just the taste of them promises you almost perfect bliss. "A thousand billion thousand portholes," as Tintin's friend, Captain Haddock, would probably have said!

Preparation time: 10 minutes
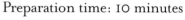
- Oil for frying
- 6 oz (150 g) uncooked shrimp
- 2 tbsp whiskey
- Salt and pepper

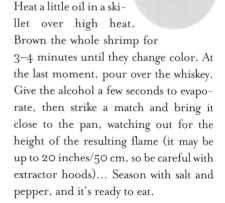

Heat a little oil in a skillet over high heat. Brown the whole shrimp for 3–4 minutes until they change color. At the last moment, pour over the whiskey. Give the alcohol a few seconds to evaporate, then strike a match and bring it close to the pan, watching out for the height of the resulting flame (it may be up to 20 inches/50 cm, so be careful with extractor hoods)… Season with salt and pepper, and it's ready to eat.

Unconventional salad

There's nothing like ridding yourself of old habits for helping you to escape from conventional ideas, traditionally acceptable codes of behavior, and pre-determined roles! For example, stop using lettuce—it's nothing special—and use flat-leaf parsley in salads… Be where you're not expected. Surprise yourself before anyone else by making these changes.

Preparation time: 10 minutes

- 1 bunch flat-leaf parsley (about 1/4 lb/100 g)
- 2 tbsp sunflower oil
- 1 tbsp cider vinegar (or white wine vinegar)
- 1 buffalo mozzarella
- 1 small pot green tapenade
- 4 or 5 anchovy fillets

Wash and dry the parsley. Cut off the stems, keeping only the leaves. Arrange the parsley leaves on a plate. Drizzle with the oil and vinegar. Cut a few slices of mozzarella. Cover these with a thin layer of green tapenade, then arrange the anchovy fillets on top and eat with the salad.

Note

Don't use olive oil instead of sunflower oil, as it tends to overwhelm the taste of the vinegar. The green tapenade may be replaced by black tapenade, but don't overdo it. Its stronger taste would wipe out the flavor of the flat-leaf parsley.

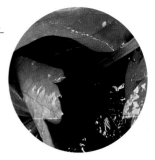

Flamed lobster with pastis

Desperate situations call for desperate measures... Ditch your frozen foods, take a walk around the market and come face to face with your favorite fish merchant's live merchandise. Lobsters cost a small fortune, but after all, didn't you ever treat yourselves to one when you were still a couple? No? Well, put things right now, and play at being a ravenous gourmet bitten by the vice of greed. You won't regret it. Besides, you have no regrets, have you?

Preparation time: 20 minutes

· 1 live lobster
· A few sprigs of fennel
· 2 tsp salted butter
· 3 tbsp pastis

Preheat the oven to its highest setting. Cut the lobster in half lengthwise while still alive and remove the sandy sac. Place flesh side up in a large heatproof dish. Cover with sprigs of fennel and small cubes of butter, then bake in the oven for 7 minutes. Heat the pastis in a pan, pour over the lobster just as you take it out of the oven, then take a lighted match to it to flame it.

Note

To make the lobster easier to cut up, put it in the freezer for 30 minutes to anesthetize it. Alternatively, plunge it in boiling water for a few minutes to kill it, then continue with the recipe, reducing the cooking time in the oven.

Korean rösti

You're fed up with potatoes, you know them inside and out, you never want to see one again, and just thinking about them makes you feel almost like continuing your hunger strike. But the pangs are gnawing at you and potatoes are the only edible thing left in your cupboards… Anyong!* Here is a Korean version of rösti that will freshen up your ideas about tubers and provide central heating for your mouth. Beware, lovers of traditional French cooking should keep away.

* Cheers!

For the rösti

- I onion
- 1/2 lb (250 g) potatoes
- I egg
- I tbsp Maïzena or cornstarch
- 2 tbsp oil
- Salt and pepper

For the sauce

- I tsp white sesame seeds
- I garlic clove
- I scallion
- I tsp superfine sugar
- 2 tbsp Korean soy sauce
- 1/2 tbsp mirin (Korean rice wine)
- 1/2 tbsp sesame oil
- 1/2 tsp chopped red chili pepper

Preparation time:
40 minutes

Start by making the sauce. Toast the sesame seeds by dry-frying in a small skillet until golden. Be careful, this can happen very quickly! Allow to cool in a bowl for 5 minutes. Chop the garlic finely. Slice the scallion very thinly. Add the sugar, soy sauce, mirin, sesame oil, garlic, scallion, and chili to the bowl. Set aside in a sauceboat or a small bowl.

For the rösti: Chop the onion finely. Wash and peel the potatoes, and grate with a medium grater. Beat the egg and Maïzena or cornstarch together in a bowl. When the mixture is smooth, add the onion and potatoes. Season with salt and pepper. Heat the oil in a large skillet over high heat (but not too high, otherwise the

rösti will be burnt on the outside and undercooked on the inside). Put a large tablespoon of potato mixture in the pan and flatten slightly into a cake. Fry gently for 2–3 minutes, then turn over using a spatula and cook for an additional 2 minutes. Cook all the rösti together if the pan is big enough, otherwise in batches. Serve very hot with a plain green salad, and dip in the accompanying sauce.

Risotto with sage

There are as many risotto recipes as there are Italians, but this one recalls the splendid Grazia, the gentle but indomitable heroine of Emanuele Crialese's movie *Respiro*. Like her, this dish is simple yet untamed, inspiring us to make a bid for freedom with its powerful, peppery sage, crisp, salty ham, intoxicating spices, and smooth, creamy rice. A recipe to make part of your repertoire, and a movie to see (again).

Preparation time: 30 minutes

· Generous 1 cup (250 ml) vegetable (or chicken) stock
· 10 sage leaves
· 1 generous pinch freshly ground nutmeg
· 1/2 onion
· 4 tsp butter
· Scant 1/3 cup (60 g) Italian short-grain rice
· 2 tbsp mild olive oil
· 2 thin slices jambon cru or prosciutto
· A few Parmesan shavings
· Salt and pepper

In a pan, bring the stock to a boil with 3 sage leaves and the nutmeg. Turn off the heat and allow to infuse. Peel the half onion and chop finely. Brown in 1 teaspoon butter over low heat until transparent. Add the rice, stirring continuously until the rice turns golden. Pour over half the sage stock, while continuing to stir. When the rice has absorbed all the liquid, pour in the remaining stock, continuing to stir until all the liquid has been absorbed. Add the remaining butter, season with salt and pepper, and stir. In a large skillet, heat the olive oil and fry the slices of ham. Drain, and fry the remaining sage leaves in the same oil. Serve the risotto garnished with Parmesan shavings, ham, and crispy sage leaves.

Tortellini in a rage

Remember the fury of those beautiful, passionate Italian actresses as they found out by chance about the goings on that wrecked their married lives (Anna Magnani, Sophia Loren, Monica Bellucci…)? Allow yourself to behave like them and go through all the stages of anger, while still opting for elegance and style in the kitchen!

Preparation time: 20 minutes

· 3 ripe tomatoes
· 1 sprig of basil
· 1 sprig of fresh thyme
· 1 or 2 small fresh red chili peppers
· 1 small onion
· 1 garlic clove
· 2 tbsp olive oil
· 4–5 oz (125 g) tortellini
· A few Parmesan shavings
· Salt and pepper

Wash the tomatoes, basil, thyme, and chili(es). Remove the seeds from the tomatoes and dice small. Peel and slice the onion. Chop the garlic and chili very small (beware! wear gloves). In a skillet, heat the olive oil and brown the onion and chili for 3 minutes, until the onion is slightly golden and transparent. Add the tomatoes, thyme, and garlic. Season with salt and pepper, cover, and cook for 10 minutes. Meanwhile, cook the tortellini in plenty of boiling salted water. Serve the tortellini covered with the sauce and garnished with chopped basil and Parmesan shavings.

Iced melon with ginger syrup

The sun is at its height, the shutters are closed on a clenched stomach and a broken heart. You need a bite of something sweet, sugary, and poisonous before flopping down for a siesta that, sadly, will remain totally decorous. This dessert is planned to help you enjoy the stimulation of the cool, fresh fruit and the enchantment of the hot spices.

Preparation: 20 min.

- 1/2 melon
- 1/4 inch (0.5 cm) piece of fresh gingerroot
- 2 tbsp superfine sugar
- 1/2 cinnamon stick

Put the melon in the refrigerator the evening before. On the day, peel and chop the ginger. Place in a pan with the sugar, cinnamon, and a scant 1/2 cup (100 ml) water. Bring to a boil and simmer to make a syrup. Allow to cool. Meanwhile, scoop the seeds from the melon. Make melon balls, using a melon baller. Put the balls in a serving dish and cover with the syrup, having removed the cinnamon stick. Stir gently, and place in the freezer for 15 minutes. Stir and put back in the freezer for an additional 15 minutes before eating.

Red fruit cup with vodka

It's as quick as a conjuring trick (though nobody's trying to force you to enjoy conjuring tricks). It's also a way of disposing of that bottle of vodka that's been biding its time at the back of the freezer. Maybe your moment has come. Raise your glass and drink to your future.

Preparation time: 5 minutes

· Assorted red fruits (raspberries, blueberries, black currants, strawberries, red currants, etc.)
· Flavored vodka
· Confectioner's sugar

Place the fruits in a glass and pour over the vodka, without drowning the fruit. Dust with confectioner's sugar and eat immediately.

Chocolate orgasm

This is a tour de force, the culmination of the pleasure you get from chocolate and its sidekicks pepper and ginger, which works in two stages. The ginger arouses and excites the taste buds to start with, while the pepper keeps a kind of inner fire going that is really quite disturbing…

Preparation time: 30 minutes

· 1 3/4 oz (50 g) bittersweet chocolate
· Generous tbsp butter
· 1 egg, separated
· Superfine sugar
· 1 tbsp milk
· 2 tbsp flour, sifted
· 1 tsp chopped fresh gingerroot
· 1/2 tsp freshly ground black pepper
· Salt

Preheat the oven to 430 °F (220 °C). Butter and sugar the inside of a small ramekin and place in the refrigerator. Break the chocolate in small pieces, set aside four squares, and slowly melt the rest in a small pan with the butter. Mix well and allow to cool. Beat the egg white until stiff. In a bowl, beat the egg yolk with 1 heaping teaspoon sugar until the mixture is white and frothy.

Add the milk, the sifted flour, and a pinch of salt, then the melted chocolate. Delicately fold in the stiff egg white. Heat 1/4 cup (60 ml) water with the ginger, pepper, and 1 tablespoon sugar in a small pan, and reduce to a syrup. Remove from the heat, and when the syrup has cooled a little, add the reserved squares of chocolate and stir until smooth. If necessary, return to a low heat to melt the chocolate thoroughly. Take care not to put the chocolate in syrup that is too hot, as it will burn. Pour half the egg mixture into a ramekin. Gently pour over the spicy syrup so that it stays in the middle of the ramekin, then cover with the rest of the egg mixture. Cook in the oven for 10 minutes, until the surface starts to crack. Eat warm.

Roasted fruits with cognac

This is all about the ends of bottles that you have to finish off by yourself, so you might as well enjoy it and gently dissolve into a state of fruity, slightly sweet, intoxication (our friend Anne knows all about that). All you need is a few nice juicy seasonal fruits that in conjunction with the alcohol will produce slow but powerful amnesiac effects, which shouldn't bother you since, basically, it's all about forgetting, isn't it?

Preparation time: 15 minutes

- Nectarines, peaches, apricots, plums, or figs (whatever you like, as long as they're juicy)
- 3 tbsp cognac
- 2 tsp brown sugar
- 2 tsp pine nuts

Wash the fruits and cut in half. Place in a small gratin dish. Pour over the cognac, then sprinkle with the sugar and the pine nuts. Cook under a pre-heated broiler for 7–10 minutes. Eat warm or even very hot, with a ball of vanilla ice cream as an extra treat for the greedy ones among you.

I want loads of love

Exquisite pleasures

Have your cake and eat it

What felt like dying a little wasn't really dying—after all, you are free! You can feel a throbbing in your chest, and it's not only because you had to run to catch the bus, but because you're smiling at life and life is smiling back. With your heart trembling and full of hope, you have done the rounds of short-lived relationships and you're dreaming of a true

passion. You don't want to waste any more time on silly, vain, empty-headed people. You are almost in love with love. In short, you are ready to rejoin the grand circle of life again, but who with, and how? The game is over, everyone puts their cards on the table…

You know yourself much better now, and the ordeals you have been through have enabled you to draw serious conclusions and make big decisions. You know what you want, and above all, what you don't want. This dearly recovered freedom is not to be sold off cheap for a living hot water bottle, you want love with a capital L, but not at the price of compromise with a big fat C…

The few healing excesses that you have adopted during your "reconstruction" have taken you down a new path, and along the way your thirst for the stay-at-home life has been moderated by folly and overindulgence. You are no longer quiet and sensible, so you have decided not to worry too much about restrictions. Why choose between cream and butter? Between your faithful cat and the adorable puppy that will wave its paws at you? And why not indulge in those hypnotic tropical fish as well? Today won't last forever, and who knows if you'll still be able to enjoy this lovely sunshine if you don't picnic right now on your office roof? Two pairs of pantyhose, one on top of the other, instead of just one—it's chic, it's sporty, you can do it. Having your hair

short on one side and long on the other is stylish. We've already seen tarte Tatin and honeycake together in the same dish (p. 82). As for grand passion, since it's a long time coming, why deprive yourself of the pleasure of collecting a few substitutes here and there in the meantime? But... only a nibble, of course. Your heart is already promised.

This final stage is the trickiest, because you are cured, but almost ready to fall into the first trap you come across... The recipes in this chapter will satisfy your irrepressible need for affection with their sweetness.

Because I'm worth it

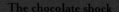

The chocolate shock
You know your own weaknesses, so this time, go round to your local cake or candy store and stock up on magnesium. After all, you need to recharge your batteries… And aspirin or vitamin C aren't going to help you recover. So give in to your desires and stop giving yourself a hard time about it. What will save you is to keep on asking for more out of life!

Soft as silk
Silky fabrics are like caresses (something you've really been missing), so don't go without any longer. Wear silk underwear, chiffon pants, a taffeta jacket, and an ostrich feather boa round your neck, a selection or all at the same time. It will make you look divine, but not like a chocolate box… Silk is so soft that it rustles gently as you move: like the sound of angels' wings.

Steam baths

If you are so overcome by exhaustion that you can't even sleep properly any more and the next vacation you've planned is a month away (and you don't know where you're going or who you're going with!), treat yourself to a day at the beauty spa and take advantage of all the treatments on offer: body scrub, facial... Now's the time to go along with your best friend, the one who knows all the latest gossip, because it's worth spending several hours there, and it's the perfect chance for philosophical chit-chat!

Be brave and look ahead

Have you never dared to read romantic fiction? There's nothing like it for curing you of the pains of love (so have no scruples about putting aside the latest gloomy intellectual novel, which will only increase your distaste for life). Read your first hospital romance or a slushy magazine, then start writing a love story of your own before you live it.

Love potion

The day you think you've met a soulmate again, concoct a love potion of your own invention for him/her: cinnamon, ginger, vanilla, cloves, red wine, and... a few drops of your precious perfume. Let the charm work.

Baby spinach with strawberries

Or how to revolutionize spinach by avoiding a forced marriage with creamy sauce in favor of a fine romance with red fruit. You get a colorful dish, elegant but not unapproachable, costing next to nothing, and with an indefinable piquancy that will leave you wanting more. That's the real you: chic, natural, and vivacious.

Preparation time: 10 minutes

- 1 large handful baby spinach leaves
- 2/3 cup (100 g) strawberries
- 1 tbsp balsamic vinegar
- A few Parmesan shavings
- 2–3 scallions
- 2 tbsp olive oil
- Salt and pepper

Wash the spinach and dry well before putting on a plate. Wash, hull, and dry the strawberries. Cut in half, or in quarters if they are big. Drizzle the spinach with the balsamic vinegar using a nice spiral motion, which in itself is enough to cheer you up. Arrange the strawberries, Parmesan shavings, and scallions (leaving them whole) over the spinach. Drizzle with olive oil. Season with salt and pepper.

Mozzarella in carrozza

At the moment you need affection in this rough world... What can you do to convince yourself that gentleness—and nothing else!—is inside you? Mozzarella, the cheese with the soft heart, can be your most dependable ally. Your taste buds and memories have already being enchanted by its milky texture and subtle flavor. When melted, it is just as captivating and will arouse all your senses, reminding you that Italy is one of the most exhilarating of all destinations—the home of Latin lovers and delightfully crazy people, and of Saverio, who gave us this recipe, and who says he likes "Spinoza, Deleuze, uncomplicated women, and the dazzling future, even by electric light."

Preparation time: 10 minutes

· 1 egg
· 4 basil leaves
· 6 oz (150 g) fresh mozzarella
· 2 sun-dried tomatoes
· 2–3 tbsp bread crumbs
· Oil for frying
· Salt and pepper

Beat the egg with salt and pepper. Wash and dry the basil leaves. Cut the mozzarella in thick slices. With a thin paring knife, make an incision in the edge so you can insert some basil and a piece of sun-dried tomato. Roll each piece in the bread crumbs, not forgetting the sides, dip in the beaten egg, then roll in the bread crumbs again. Heat a little oil in a skillet and when very hot fry the mozzarella croquettes briefly until they are soft and golden. Serve with a green salad and a few tomatoes.

Cream of pumpkin soup with hazelnut oil

The very color of pumpkin is enough to warm your heart just looking at it on display at your local market... More than any other vegetable, pumpkin and squash (it comes to the same thing, they're part of the same family) are the champion ingredients for soup as winter approaches. This soup is wonderfully golden, smooth, subtly enhanced by a bewitching nutty flavor, with strange powers that make you feel you're regaining your inner equilibrium... or maybe it's just a flavor of childhood.

Preparation time: 30 minutes

· 2 small carrots
· 1/2 lb (250 g) pumpkin
· 1 tsp butter
· 2/3 cup (150 ml) vegetable or chicken stock
· 1 tbsp chopped flat-leaf parsley
· Hazelnut oil
· 3 hazelnuts (or walnuts), chopped
· Salt and pepper

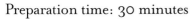

Wash and peel the vegetables. Cut the carrots in rounds and the pumpkin in cubes. Melt the butter in a sauté pan and fry the carrots gently for 5 minutes. Add the pumpkin and cover. Let the vegetables soften for 10 minutes, stirring occasionally. Add the vegetable or chicken stock and 1 tablespoon chopped flat-leaf parsley. Season with salt and pepper. Process in a blender and drizzle with a dash of hazelnut oil. Garnish with the chopped nuts and a few chopped parsley leaves.

Carrot soup with cilantro

While the English get their children to eat carrots by saying they help you see in the dark, the French say that carrots make you lovable. The first definition of this adjective in the dictionary is "worthy of love," so they will certainly do you good. Serve them raw or cooked, as an appetizer, a main dish, or even as a dessert, if you like carrot cake. Just a touch of cilantro is enough to carry you up beyond the stratosphere.

Preparation time: 30 minutes

· 10 baby carrots, about 6 oz (150 g)
· 1 small potato
· 1/2 onion
· 1 tbsp butter
· Oil
· Generous 1 cup (250 ml) hot vegetable or chicken stock
· 1 tsp ground coriander
· 1 tsp chopped fresh cilantro
· 1 tbsp chopped celery leaves
· Salt and pepper

Wash, peel, and dice the carrots and the potato. Chop the half onion and brown gently in a large saucepan with 2 teaspoons butter and a drop of oil. When the onion has turned transparent, add the potato, then the carrots. Cover and allow to soften for 10 minutes over low heat. Add the hot stock, bring to a boil and simmer for an additional 10 minutes. Melt the remaining butter in a small skillet and brown the ground coriander for 1 minute, stirring continuously. Add the chopped celery leaves and cilantro and cook for an additional minute. Pour this mixture into the saucepan and mix everything together. Season with salt and pepper, and garnish with celery leaves to add a touch of color.

Variations: To make the soup creamier, add 1/3 cup (75 ml) milk before mixing everything together; to make it more invigorating, add a few drops of lemon juice.

Zucchini soup with a black currant coulis

Give in to the temptation of this combination of a vegetable, an aromatic herb, and the flesh of a fruit that has the reputation of being tricky to use in cooking. But in this phase, when you are getting going again, all things are possible, and the idea of setting yourself new challenges energizes you with a strange passion. All the ingredients are available all year round (you should be able to buy bottled or frozen coulis). This is the perfect recipe for rescuing you from a miserable evening, thanks to its magical colors, their effect heightened by the combination of flavors.

Preparation time: 20 minutes

- 1 tsp sea salt
- 1/2 vegetable bouillon cube
- 2 large zucchini (or 3 small ones)
- 5 basil leaves
- 2 tbsp sour cream
- 1 tbsp black currant coulis

Add the sea salt to a saucepan of water, bring to a boil and drop in the half bouillon cube. Wash the zucchini and cut in small pieces without peeling (all the flavor is in the skins). Plunge them in the boiling water. Cook for 10–15 minutes, depending on the size of the pieces. Drain the zucchini, reserving the stock, and process in a blender. Chop the basil leaves and add them to the zucchini in the blender, then with the blender running add sufficient stock to obtain the desired consistency. Before eating, swirl over the sour cream and black currant coulis.

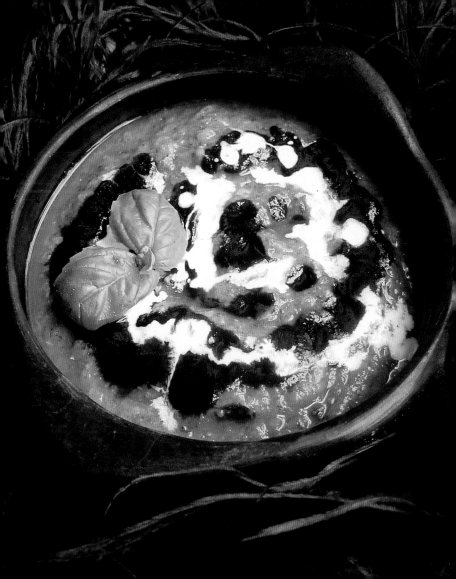

Violet cake

A quick glance in the rear-view mirror to console the child in you, still smarting from a wounded ego. Your heartache will vanish with each mouthful of this treat made by my Breton grandmother, who gets out her good old Calvados as a miracle cure for boils, stiff necks, and the pains of love. Honey and flowers to sugar the pill, and my feet start tapping in time to the music…

supercalifragilisticexpialidocious!

Preparation time: 45 minutes

· Scant 3 tbsp salted butter + 1 teaspoon for the cake pan
· 5/8 cup (70 g) flour, sifted + 1 tsp for the cake pan
· 1/4 cup (80 g) honey
· Scant 1 tbsp violet petal conserve
· 1 egg
· 2 tbsp milk
· 1/4 cup (30 g) buckwheat flour, sifted
· 1 tsp baking powder
· 1 tsp Calvados
· About 10 candied violets

Preheat the oven to 430 °F (220 °C). Butter and flour a small cake pan (a rectangular loaf pan will do fine). In a saucepan, slowly melt the honey, butter (in small pieces), and the violet petal conserve, to give a smooth mixture. Break the egg into a bowl, beat it and incorporate first the milk, then the sifted flours and the baking powder. Pour in the honey mixture and mix. Pour into the prepared cake pan and bake in the oven for 25 –30 minutes. Turn out while warm and sprinkle with candied violets. Can be eaten warm or cold.

Note

What? You haven't any violet petal conserve to hand? Check out the website www.maisondelaviolette.fr or order it, for example from www.leschantsduterroir.com.

Grapefruit curd

You're leading a high-speed life, and as you rush ahead, you often don't find time to sit down to eat. Is that a good reason for eating any old rubbish? Here is a sweet spread you can eat on its own at any time of day, at breakfast, as an improvised dessert, or on a slice of bread, so you can keep a little bubble of pleasure inside you, just for yourself, and enjoy the present, just for a moment.

Preparation time: 30 minutes

· 1 small untreated lemon
· 1/2 grapefruit
· 3 egg yolks
· Scant 1/2 cup (100 g) superfine sugar
· 6 tbsp butter, straight from the refrigerator

Wash the lemon in hot water. Dry carefully, and grate the zest into thin shavings. Squeeze the half grapefruit and the lemon, and strain the juice. Beat the egg yolks and sugar in a pan till light and frothy. Stir in the fruit juice and grated zest, heat gently (do not allow to boil) until the mixture thickens to a cream. Cut the well-chilled butter in cubes. Remove the pan from the heat and drop in the cubes of butter a few at a time. Beat until the mixture cools. Pour into sterilized jars and seal immediately. Allow to cool and store in the refrigerator.

Dad's dessert

When you're ten years old and you see your father cooking for the first time in your life, you automatically assume that he's only a beginner. You're a bit curious, but mainly greedy. You watch, you take note, you tease him a bit and then, when you see what's going into this tart, you wrinkle up your nose at the thought of having to eat it. This beautiful pastry that has been kneaded so lovingly and competently (well, there's a surprise) is about to be spoiled by a strange mixture that would go much better with mushrooms... But children get forgiven, because making hasty judgments is all part of being young and foolish.

Preparation time: 20 minutes

- Butter
- Short crust pastry
- 2 tbsp crème fraîche or sour cream
- I tbsp superfine sugar
- I pinch salt
- I tbsp raspberry vinegar

Preheat the oven to 440 ° F (225 °C). Butter a small tart pan (about 6 inches/15 cm diameter) and sprinkle with sugar. Lay the pastry in it and prick with a small fork. In a bowl, beat together the crème fraîche or sour cream, sugar, salt, and vinegar. Cover the pastry with it and cook in the oven for 15 minutes, until golden brown. This dessert may be eaten warm or cold.

Baked apple with cider cream

This is like a dessert from the good old days, long past. Make it with cider or barley beer, whichever you prefer. Get back to your roots, and draw on the old-fashioned spirit of endurance in the face of adversity. But that sort of endurance is also associated with comforting memories of good traditional food, bringing to mind your stomach rather than the battlefield.

Preparation time: 20 minutes

- 1 apple
- 1 tsp lemon juice
- 1 tsp crème fraîche or sour cream
- 1 tbsp hard cider
- 1 pinch ground cinnamon
- 2 tsp brown sugar
- 1/2 vanilla bean
- 1 slice bread
- Butter

Preheat the oven to 465 °F (240 °C). Wash the apple and cut across the base so it will stand straight. Remove the core with an apple corer. In a bowl, mix the lemon juice, crème fraîche or sour cream, cider, cinnamon, and brown sugar. Pour this mixture into the apple and insert the half vanilla bean cut lengthwise. Place the apple on a slice of buttered bread. Bake in the oven for 15 minutes. The apple will be soft and slightly caramelized.

How this book was born

Claire and Marina are my neighbors on the same floor, in their thirties, married, and with children (that creates bonds). One of them suddenly suffered the same experience that the other had been through a few years before-

claire.jacquet@free.fr

re, but from the other side: when couples separate, one of them often stays behind and the other leaves. Marina immediately initiated Claire into the secrets of the aromas and flavors that can refocus and rebuild flagging morale and help you to find yourself again. A straight-forward yet wise theory that is quickly proved to be correct.

mveuillet@wanadoo.fr

That was the starting point for this book, which is permeated as much by actual experience of breaking up as by talking about it (men, women, blah blah blah…). The sixth floor of a Parisian apartment block became a hive of feverish activity and pots, pans, and spoons flew around, while a publisher soon got onto it and seemed to think it would be a bestseller…

So I would like to thank the following for their warmth and friendship and for confiding in me: Anne Arregui, Béatrice Cherpitel, Noémie Cohen, François Curlet, Patrick Debusschère, Florence Doléac, Claire Dubois, Yvonne Fresneau, Claire Guézengar, Marie-Madeleine Jacquet, Benoît Lecarpentier, Maurice Lecomte, Pierre Leguillon, Sébastien Leroy, Guillemette Lorin, Saverio Lucariello, Bernard Mathonnat, Ariane Michel, Alexis Mosset, Gianni Motti, Cédric Protière, Anne Roumet, Maï Tran, Rémi Vandome, Carlos Velez de Villa and Simon Veuillet, as well as Florent Guézengar, for recalling his favorite romantic movies.